TABLE OF CONTENTS

Page

ABBREVIATIONS

ACH	Alternate Competing Hypotheses
CCP	Chinese Communist Party
CRS	Congressional Research Service
DGDP	Directorate of Graduate Degree Programs
FARC	Revolutionary Armed Forces of Colombia
GDP	Graduate Degree Programs
GOC	Government-owned Company
INCSR	International Narcotics Control Strategy Report
PLA	People's Liberation Army
PRC	People's Republic of China
RMA	Revolution in Military Affairs
SGA	Small Group Advisor
SWOT	Strength, Weakness, Opportunity, and Threat
TBA	Tri-Border Area
TOC	Transnational Organized Crime
UNODC	United Nations Office on Drug and Crime

ILLUSTRATIONS

TABLES

CHAPTER 1

INTRODUCTION

Where the borders of Argentina, Brazil, and Paraguay converge lies a region known as the Tri-Border Area (TBA). Geographically defined by the Parana and Iguazu Rivers, the TBA is strategically located along the Pan American Highway and has become a major center for commerce. Here, operating within a heterogeneous population of more than 700,000 people, specific groups compete to fulfill seemingly disparate objectives.[1]

Crowded into three major population centers–the Argentine city of Puerto Iguazu, the Brazilian city of Foz do Iguacu, and the Paraguayan city of Ciudad del Este (Figure 1) the current TBA population is ethnically diverse. In addition to the native Argentine, Brazilian, and Paraguayan populations, as of 2001 approximately 30,000 Chinese inhabit the area, up from the much smaller number of 6,500 in 1994.[2] Moreover, the region has a sizable Arab population including Palestinian and Lebanese nationals reportedly numbering around 23,000.[3]

Although the TBA arguably exists unnoticed by the world-at-large, the region acts as a busy conduit for commerce. The Brazilian and Paraguayan governments established a free-trade zone during the 1970s in order to promote economic growth. Ciudad del Este has become the world's third largest market, after Hong Kong and Miami.[4] On any given day, 30,000 people will cross the Friendship Bridge between Brazil and Paraguay, engaged in both legitimate and illicit trade. Most of that illicit trade involves trafficking in narcotics by groups unfriendly to the U.S. and generally proceeds with impunity. "Narcotics' trafficking has an estimated cash flow equivalent to 50 percent of Paraguay's gross domestic product (US$8.1 billion)."[5] Quite simply, the TBA "provides a haven that is geographically, socially, economically, and politically highly conducive for allowing the activities of organized crime, Islamic terrorist groups, and corrupt officials" to flourish unimpeded in spite of serious efforts by the federal governments of Argentina, Brazil, and Paraguay.[6]

Source: Americas on NBCNEWS.com, www.ndcnews.com/id/17874369/ns/world_news-americas/t/hezbollah-builds-western-base/#.Ubf_mpVgPzl (accessed May 15, 2013).

Since the establishment of the TBA as a free trade zone in the 1970s, porous borders, existing smuggling routes, and widespread local and regional corruption have enabled transnational organized crime and terrorist organizations to exploit this duty-free zone.[7] Such exploitation has negative consequences for both the general population of the

TBA not involved in illegitimate activities and for the U.S. due to the transnational nature of narcotics trafficking.

Narco-trafficking links production to consumption. The TBA is an active narco-trafficking corridor where opiates and precursor chemicals, originating in South East Asia, are destined for U.S. markets. Additionally, cocaine, originating in the Andean region, is destined for European markets. According to the United Nations Office on Drugs and Crime's *World Drug Report* in 2012, the United States continued to be the largest consumer of illegal drugs.[8] As a result, the economic and social problems created equate to over US$ 200 billion for treatment associated with substance abuse and an estimated loss in productivity of one per cent of GDP.[9] Unfortunately, narco-trafficking continues to be highly profitable.

Since the Nixon administration declared a "war on drugs" in 1971, the U.S. has maintained a clear strategy on drug control.

> Transnational criminal threats and illicit trafficking networks continue to expand dramatically in size, scope, and influence–posing significant national security challenges for the United States and our partner countries. These threats cross borders and continents and undermine the stability of nations, subverting government institutions through corruption and harming citizens worldwide. Transnational criminal organizations have accumulated unprecedented wealth and power through trafficking and other illicit activities, penetrating legitimate financial systems and destabilizing commercial markets. They extend their reach by forming alliances with government officials and some state security services.[10]

Terrorist organizations have increasingly turned to narcotics trafficking for funding their activities, which may be directed towards the United States and others. For example, Paraguayan authorities thwarted a plot to attack the U.S. and Israeli embassies in 2000.[11] U.S. Southern Command in 2003 estimated "that Islamic fundamentalist groups in the TBA and similar areas in Latin America are sending between US$300 million and US$500 million a year in profits from drug trafficking, arms dealing, and other illegal activities, including money laundering, contraband, and product piracy, to radical Islamic groups in the Middle East."[12]

"Islamic terrorist groups with a presence in the TBA reportedly include Egypt's Al-Gama'a al-Islamiyya (Islamic Group) and Al-Jihad (Islamic Jihad), al Qaeda, Hamas, Hizballah, and al-Muqawamah (the Resistance; also spelled al-Moqawamah), which is a pro-Iran wing of the Lebanon-based Hizballah."[13] All of these groups more or less participate in drug trafficking, money laundering, and recruiting, their activities supported and/or sanctioned by local officials who accept their bribes or payoffs, content to persist in a symbiotic relationship of corruption.

The inability of the Paraguayan, Brazilian, and Argentine governments to solve the problems that currently plague the region can be partially attributed to wide spread corruption at the local and state levels. The U.S. Department of State's 2009 International Narcotics Control Strategy Report (INCSR) indicated that Paraguay was a primary money laundering center due to weak financial controls and the ease of cross-border transfer of currency.[14] In July 2000, "former Paraguayan General Lino Oviedo" reportedly "laundered about US$10 million through money transfer operations from Foz do Iguacu to Ciudad del Este."[15] Existing conditions of widespread corruption and ineffective state institutions have further enabled criminal operations throughout Paraguay.[16]

In addition to terrorist organizations actively operating within the TBA, transnational criminal organizations are prevalent as well. Regional security forces confirm that non-indigenous mafias operating in the TBA include those from China.

4

Chinese mafias have had a presence in the TBA since the 1990s.[17] According to Paraguayan police, at least six different Chinese organized crime syndicates conduct illicit and/or illegal activities in the TBA. These mafias include the Fuk Ching, Pac Lun Fu, Tai Chen Sananh, Continental, the Big Circle Boys, and the Flying Dragons.[18] Security forces of Argentina, Brazil, and Paraguay in 2000 assessed that that these transnational organized crime syndicates collected around US$30,000 per month.[19] Moreover, these groups are "known to collaborate with Islamic terrorist groups in the region."[20]

Such a strong presence of transnational organized crime in the TBA is a constant danger to the stability of the region and a major security threat to the United States as outlined by the President in his 2011 Strategy to Combat Transnational Organized Crime. American interests in Latin America have remained mostly unchanged for the past several decades: strengthen security, advance democracy, and encourage economic growth. Narcotics trafficking and the locally acceptable presence of transnational organized crime in the TBA make it all but impossible for the U.S. to advance these interests. Narco-trafficking has a destabilizing effect on the region through the use of violent acts directed towards the government or population. Moreover, drug trafficking organizations are now operating in the United States to ensure illegal drugs reach U.S. markets. Drug trafficking in particular creates a pernicious atmosphere that is hard to overcome.

The 2011 U.S. National Drug Control Strategy highlights the importance of assisting international partners in order to defeat drug trafficking operations and defend against the growing global security threat posed by transnational organized crime.[21] The

U.S. currently supports both bilateral and multilateral engagements in the TBA, which address financial crime and counter-terrorism financing. However, these are U.S.-Latin American partnerships.

The operations of terrorist organizations and transnational organized crime represent a growing security threat in and among themselves. The addition of an increasing Chinese presence in the region further adds to the complexity of the strategic environment due to competing national interests. China has become a key trading partner in the region over the past decade. According to a 2011 *Asian Times* article, "Sino-Latin American trade has risen from US$12 billion in 2000 to more than US$140 billion," overtaking the United States as the top trading partner.[22]

China seems to be actively (and nefariously) pursuing an economic advantage. Chinese investments often resulted in "guarantees of access to certain natural resources."[23] In 2009, Brazil and Argentina received US$10 billion in loans from China.[24] Subsequently, China gained access to energy exports. Additionally, Latin America offers the Chinese a growing consumer market. Furthermore, Latin America's dependence on the Chinese economy translates into an increase of influence in the region.

> China's increased involvement in Latin America is part of its long-term grand strategy. This strategy focuses on "comprehensive national power" necessary to achieve the status of a "global great power that is second to none" by 2049. It seeks energy security and access to natural resources, raw materials, and overseas markets to sustain its economic expansion. It pursues military power and aims to build a network of Beijing's friends and allies through China's "soft power" and diplomatic charm offensive, trade, and economic dependencies via closer economic integration and mutual security pacts, intelligence cooperation, and arms sales.[25]

The Chinese have progressively inserted themselves in Latin America where "China is seen as an opportunity for Latin America to break the existing North-South asymmetry, forging friendships among neighboring countries."[26]

Nevertheless, "the activities of Chinese mafia groups create an inherent criminal link between China and Latin America, insofar as threats against families in China are often used as one of the tools for extorting Chinese individuals in Latin America."[27] The opportunistic nature of transnational organized crime goes far beyond extortion, including: human trafficking, narcotics trafficking, trafficking of contraband, arms trafficking, and money laundering.[28] The increasing illegal and legitimate ties between China and Latin America warrant further investigation into determining whether or not this activity is coincidental or intentional on the part of the Chinese Government as global trends indicates that with the increase of Chinese investments in developing countries influence the emergence of Chinese transnational organized crime.

Definitions

For the purpose of this study, narco-terrorism will be defined as "terrorist acts carried out by groups that are directly or indirectly involved in cultivating, manufacturing, transporting, or distributing illicit drugs."[29] "The term is also applied to groups that use the drug trade to fund terrorist organizations."[30]

The National Security Council defines transnational organized crime as "those self-perpetuating associations of individuals who operate transnationally for the purpose of obtaining power, influence, monetary and/or commercial gains, wholly or in part by illegal means, while protecting their activities through a pattern of corruption and/or violence, or while protecting their illegal activities through a transnational organizational

7

structure and the exploitation of transnational commerce or communication mechanisms."[31]

Terrorism will be defined as "premeditated, politically motivated violence perpetrated against noncombatant targets by subnational groups or clandestine agents" contained in Title 22 of the United States Code, Section 2656f(d)(2).[32]

The Research Question

Does the Chinese government support narco-terrorism in the Tri-Border Area, which poses a threat to U.S. security objectives in Latin America?

Scope

The study pertained to this thesis was limited to the activities of terrorist organizations and transnational criminal organizations engaging in illicit trafficking operations as well as Chinese interests in the Tri-Border Area.

Limitations

Study pertaining to this thesis has inherent limitations such as limited reporting on racketeering within the relatively closed ethnic Chinese communities in the TBA and limited reporting on internal corruption on Chinese government owned companies operating in Latin America. Additional research may be required in order to adequately address and define the relationships between China and groups involved with narco-terrorism. Such research findings may not be available using open source information.

The Role of This Thesis

The emphasis of this thesis is to further explore the complex relationship between transnational organized crime, terrorist organizations, and the criminal ties between

China and Latin America while identifying possible explanations to Chinese interests in developing countries and the means Beijing will employ to secure China's global role. The hypothesis that the Chinese government is supporting narco-terrorism is based on the emergence of transnational criminal organizations in areas of increased Chinese investments such as Africa and Latin America. The TBA offers the necessary conditions for supporting such activities–porous borders, weak state institutions, and corruption. This study set out to either prove or disprove this hypothesis. Both solutions to the hypothesis present their own strategic implications for the United States. Currently, there is limited literature available that has had its primary objective to describe these linkages and discuss possible threats to U.S. security objectives in Latin America. This thesis will fill that void.

This chapter provided an introduction and established the purpose of this study. The next chapter will review key points and general themes of current literature as well as provide theoretical and methodological support for the convergence of transnational criminal organizations and terrorist organizations in the TBA compounded by growing Chinese economic interests in the region.

---

[1]Laverne Berry, Glenn E. Curtis, Rex A. Hudson, and Nina A. Kollars, *A Global Overview of Narcotics-Funded Terrorist and Other Extremist Groups* (Washington, DC: Library of Congress, 2002), 174.

[2]Ibid.

[3]Ibid.

[4]Ibid.

[5]Joshua T. Hoffman, "Tri-Border Area (TBA)," Ridgway Research, http://research.ridgway.pitt.edu/blog/2012/05/15/tri-border-area-tba/ (accessed May 10, 2013).

[6]Berry et al., 172.

[7]Ibid.

[8]UNODC, World Drug Report 2012 (United Nations publication, Sales No. E.12.XI.1, 2012), 4.

[9]Ibid.

[10]The White House, *2010 National Security Strategy* (Washington, DC: The White House, 2010), 49.

[11]Rex Hudson, *Terrorist and Organized Crime Groups in the Tri-Border Area (TBA) of South America* (Washington, DC: Library of Congress, 2003), 18.

[12]Ibid., 4.

[13]Ibid., 1.

[14]John Boote, *A Criminal Haven: The Tri-Border Area of South America*, May 11, 2009, traccc.gmu.edu/pdfs/student_research/John%20Boote-%20A%20Criminal%20 Haven.pdf (accessed May 15, 2013), 10.

[15]Ibid.

[16]Ibid.

[17]Hudson, 40.

[18]Ibid., 41.

[19]Ibid.

[20]Ibid., 42.

[21]The White House, *2011 National Drug Control Strategy* (Washington, DC: The White House, 2011), 71.

[22]Sebastian Castaneda, "South America Awake to Risks of China Ties," *Asian Times*, http://www.atimes.com/atimes/China/MD21Ad01.html (accessed April 8, 2013).

[23]Ibid.

[24]Ibid.

[25]Jane Hulse, "China's Expansion Into and U.S. Withdrawal from Argentina's Telecommunications and Space Industries and the Implications for U.S. National Security" (Strategic Studies Institute, Carlisle, PA, 2007).

[26]Ibid., 38.

[27]R. Evan Ellis, "Chinese Organized Crime in Latin America," *PRISM* 4, no. 1 (December 2012), www.ndu.edu/press/chinese-organized-crime.html (accessed May 10, 2013): 66-75.

[28]Ibid.

[29]Alvaro de Souza Pinheiro, JSOU Report 06-4, *Narcoterrorism in Latin America: A Brazilian Perspective* (Hurlburt Field, FL: Joint Special Operations University, April 2006), 11.

[30]Ibid.

[31]The White House, "Strategy to Combat Transnational Organized Crime: Definition," National Security Council, www.whitehouse.gov/administration/eop/nsc/transnational-crime/definition (accessed May 26, 2013).

[32]Terrorism FAQs, www.cia.gov/news-information/cia-the-war-on-terrorism/terrorism-faqs.html (accessed May 26, 2013).

CHAPTER 2

LITERATURE REVIEW

The purpose of this research was to determine if relationships exist between the Chinese government, transnational organized crime, and terrorist organizations within the Tri-Border Area of South America and identify possible strategic implications of the same. The research question selected is: Does the Chinese government support narco-terrorism in the Tri-Border Area which poses a threat to U.S. security objectives in Latin America? The previous chapter introduced the context of the study. This chapter will review key points and general themes of current literature including findings as well as theoretical and methodological support for the convergence of transnational criminal organizations and terrorist organizations in the TBA compounded by growing Chinese economic interests in the region.

Relationships between the Chinese government, transnational organized crime, and Latin America have not prompted the production of a large volume of research, primarily focusing on the constituent topics. Sources were selected to provide a broad point of view. However, reports prepared by the Federal Research Division of the Library of Congress published in 2002 and 2003 provided a detailed assessment of the activities of transnational crime, terrorist organizations, and narcotics trafficking in the TBA since 1999. Moreover, adequate reference material was available on the individual topics.

The Congressional Research Service (CRS), a highly respected agency providing policy and legal analysis to Members of Congress, in 2003 produced two studies of interest: *Terrorist and Organized Crime Groups in the Tri-Border Area (TBA) of South America* and *A Global Overview of Narcotics-Funded Terrorist and Other Extremist*

Groups. These were used as a factual base in order to establish the conditions existing within the TBA.

These studies provided evidence, through open-source information, that terrorist organizations use the TBA "for fund-raising, recruiting, plotting terrorist attacks elsewhere in the TBA countries or the Americas in general."[1] Additionally, they supported the idea that the TBA provides the ideal conditions for the support of transnational criminal organizations which "are known to use the TBA for illicit activities such as smuggling, money laundering, and product piracy."[2] Hudson also provides key insight to the efforts of regional security forces to counter these activities. For these reasons, the Congressional Research Service studies serve as the foundation of this study.

"The Emerging Threat of Illicit Drug Funding of Terrorist Organizations" by LTC Reaves and "Disrupting Threat Finances: Utilization of Financial Information to Disrupt Terrorist Organizations in the Twenty-First Century" by MAJ Anderson produced by the U.S. Army War College and the School of Advanced Military Studies respectfully, identified common methods that organizations involved in illicit activities utilize, both illegitimate and legitimate, in order to further their agendas. In addition, these studies identified an established link between terrorist groups and narcotics trafficking. These studies refer to the efforts of surrogates using drugs as a weapon in order to threaten the stability of free market countries. However, these two studies offered limited information regarding Chinese-Latin American criminal ties.

While all of the sources above are valuable in and of themselves, general literature on China-Latin America criminal ties is scarce with few direct sources to draw from. However, R. Evan Ellis's "Chinese Organized Crime in Latin America" demonstrates that criminal ties between China and Latin America are "an increasingly problematic by-product of expanding China-Latin America interactions" and have strategic "implications for both regions."[3] "Chinese Organized Crime in Latin America" brings to light the transnational organized criminal ties between Latin America and China. Ellis utilized both interviews and open-source data in order to uncover evidence of extortion and illicit trafficking of persons, narcotics, and contraband. Ellis argues that these criminal ties are a "natural artifact" resulting from an increased Chinese economic presence in the region.[4] He also provides implications for both Latin America and the United States. Ellis argues that Latin American security forces are under resourced to counter such threats more effectively. As for the United States, he argues that both "ethnic Chinese" and "precursor chemicals" originating from China are trafficked through the TBA and are "destined for the United States."[5] He also adds that money laundering operations involving Chinese banks support "cartels" in both Mexico and Columbia.[6] Ellis also predicts that arms trafficking and money laundering are on the rise. What drives this increase in commerce and investments between China and Latin America?

Multiple books and articles were chosen in order to establish why Beijing is increasing Chinese presence in Latin America, specifically the TBA. *China Debates the Future Security Environment* by Michael Pillsbury attempts to explain Chinese strategic thinking. Pillsbury provides viewpoints of Chinese authors, published from 1994-1999, regarding the future security environment. *China Debates the Future Security Environment* highlights differences among orthodox and reformist authors about multipolarization, the decline of U.S. power, future powers, the roles of Russia and

Japan, and future wars. Moreover, Pillsbury offers insight into China's willingness to exploit future revolutions in military affairs. While multiple arguments exist, the commonality among them is the necessity to counter a more technologically advanced military, such as the United States, using asymmetric means. In addition, a wealth of Chinese political literature in general suggests that regional conflicts will arise as the world transitions to a multipolar security environment and that economic resources will soon become the primary cause of conflict among major powers.

A recent *Foreign Affairs* article, "How China Sees America: The Sum of Beijing's Fears" coauthored by Andrew J. Nathan and Andrew Scobell published in October 2012, offers a Chinese perspective on U.S. foreign policy. The authors provide a reminder of the three Chinese geopolitical imperatives of maintaining internal stability, maintain a buffer region, and prevent foreign encroachment. In addition, Nathan and Scobell discuss what they see as a fourth threat to China–access to global markets and investment. Moreover, the article focuses attention to the fact that the U.S. has a presence in each posing a threat to China's rise. As a counter argument, Thomas P. M. Barnett's "When China Ruled the World," published December 21, 2010, argues that China is not seeking political control in areas of overseas investment but only influence.[7] Barnett goes on to argue, "rising dependence of foreign energy and food will slow Chinese growth down dramatically."[8] With that said, existing literature offers explanations into what may be occurring in the TBA.

Horacio Calderon's "Organized Crime and Terrorism in the Triple Border Area" introduces the concept of convergence, where the TBA provides the necessary conditions for collaboration between criminal and terrorist organizations in order to achieve their political or economic objectives. Calderon provides evidence of multiple Islamic based terrorist organizations operating in the TBA including Hizballah and Hamas. He also provides evidence of transnational criminal organizations including those originating from China as well as Russia. These groups collaborate in the TBA by conducting activities such as narco-trafficking, money laundering, arms trafficking, smuggling of contraband, and kidnapping. Moreover, Calderon offers an Argentine perspective on how interconnected these groups really are and the associated challenges of counter-terrorism in the region. However, other possible explanations on Chinese intent in the region must be considered.

While controversial, *Red Cocaine* by Joseph D. Douglass published in 1990 and *Psycho-chemical Warfare* by A. H. S. Candlin published in 1973 claims that the Chinese Communist Party has actively engaged in narco-trafficking operations. These sources provided analysis of the methods used by Communist states such as the Soviet Union and the People's Republic of China utilizing narcotics as weapons of subversion directed towards the West.

According to Douglass, as early as 1928, Mao Tse-tung developed a strategy of using opium as a weapon targeted against the Communist opposition.[9] Once mainland China was secured in 1949, Mao nationalized the production of opium and trafficking in narcotics was a formal activity of the Communist state.[10] Poppies became an instrument of national power and an effective weapon of subversion to use against the West. Douglass also argued that Chinese drug trafficking efforts directly correlated to increased consumption in the United States.[11]

Similarly, A. H. S. Candlin attempted to expose the Communist drug-offensive strategy. Stanton claims that the Chinese government developed a long-term strategy consisting of three phases by the 1950s.[12] The first phase (1950-56) focused on supporting infrastructure for domestic opium cultivation.[13] Phase two (1956-63) established drug trafficking corridors.[14] Finally, phase three (1963-1971) was the "realization of the objectives."[15] China's narcotics operation had become a political strategy toward the accomplishment of three objectives: the financing of clandestine activities, moral and physical weakening of opposing populations, and the destruction of the will of U.S. servicemen.[16] These books offered little evidence that this strategy would have continued once the objectives were realized.

Unrestricted Warfare, by Qiao Liang and Wang Xiangsui, provides insight into China's ability to wage war by non-conventional means in order to counter U.S. hegemony. *Unrestricted Warfare* was originally published in 1999 by the People's Liberation Army (PLA) and addresses how China could defeat a technologically superior military utilizing a combination of non-military war operations including, but not limited to, economic warfare, resource warfare, and terrorism. Qiao and Wang suggest that China recognizes non-military war operations as a revolution in military affairs (RMA) and in doing so China then possesses a distinct advantage over the West. But this view is at odds with more traditional Chinese strategic thinking.

Existing literature also provides insight into how countries will respond to China's growth. *The Rise of China vs. the Logic of Strategy* by Edward N. Luttwak argues that China's military and economic growth will be met with global economic resistance. Applying strategic logic, Luttwak makes predictions and discusses likely

17

outcomes of Chinese hard and soft aggression; he discusses the idea that as time goes on, Beijing will actively facilitate the trend towards multipolarity at an ever-increasing rate. Luttwak predicts that China's objective is to shape the future security environment in Beijing's favor. He provides examples in order to support his argument by highlighting the increase in natural resource exports from Brazil to China as "induced economic dependence."[17] However, it is likely that China's need for increased imports of natural resources is to maintain China's economic growth to ensure internal stability. Nevertheless, growing Chinese interests in developing countries create uncertainty concerning China's rise.

Luttwak argues that China's interests of economic growth, military growth, and increased global influence will evoke a countering response.[18] He provides examples of bilateral strategic partnerships among neighboring states in order to counter China's concurrent growth including: strategic dialogue between India and Japan focusing on intelligence cooperation, Japanese support to Vietnam's maritime forces, and a closer Japanese-Australian strategic partnership.[19] Moreover, understanding how regional neighbors will react to China's rise is vital to conceptualizing the macro geopolitical environment.

The literature used in this thesis primarily consisted of books, periodicals and investigations concerning strategy, policy, and terrorist networks engaged in illicit trafficking in order to provide a means of funding for personal and/or political gains. Conditions in the TBA due to weak institutions and corruption promote both narco-trafficking and Chinese investment strategies. Additionally, the literature reviewed supports the case for further study and provides readers with supporting documentation for the potential aggression of China in the TBA.

This chapter reviewed key points and general themes of current literature including findings as well as theoretical and methodological support to narco-terrorism and Chinese interests in the TBA. Additionally, the literature review supported continued research into this study. The following chapter will outline the research methodology used in this study.

---

[1]Hudson, 1.

[2]Ibid., 3.

[3]Ellis, "Chinese Organized Crime in Latin America," 65.

[4]Ibid.

[5]Ibid., 74.

[6]Ibid.

[7]Barnett, "When China Ruled the World," www.esquire.com/features/china-political-furture-0111 (accessed May 27, 2013).

[8]Ibid.

[9]Joseph D. Douglass, *Red Cocaine: The Drugging of America and the West* (New York: Edward Harle, 1999), 13.

[10]Ibid., 1.

[11]Ibid., 13.

[12]A. H. Stanton Candlin, *Psycho-Chemical Warfare: The Chinese Communist Drug Offensive Against the West* (New Rochelle, NY: Arlington House, 1973), 195.

[13]Ibid., 195-196.

[14]Ibid.

[15]Ibid.

[16]Douglass, 13.

[17]Edward Luttwak, *The Rise of China vs. the Logic of Strategy* (Cambridge, MA: The Belknap Press of Harvard University Press, 2012), 27.

[18]Ibid., 95.

[19]Ibid., 96.

CHAPTER 3

RESEARCH METHODOLOGY

The purpose of this research was to determine if relationships exist between the Chinese government, transnational organized crime, and terrorist organizations within the Tri-Border Area of South America and identify possible strategic implications of the same. The research question selected is: Does the Chinese government support narco-terrorism in the Tri-Border Area which poses a threat to U.S. security objectives in Latin America? The previous chapter reviewed points and general themes of current literature including findings as well as theoretical and methodological support to narco-terrorism in the TBA. Conditions exist in the TBA that enables both terrorist organizations and transnational criminal organizations to conduct their operations unimpeded. Additionally, China-Latin America criminal ties are present. This chapter will outline the research methodology used in this study.

Initial research indicated Qualitative Research Methodology would best satisfy the intention of identifying possible relationships among terrorist organizations, transnational organized crime, and the Chinese government in the TBA. Operations research and systems analysis provided necessary background information. However, qualitative analysis is effective only for known data, but can serve as an indicator when "understanding the intentions and capabilities of adversaries and other foreign actors is challenging, especially when either or both are concealed."[1]

Structured analytic techniques will allow for the discovery of the unknowns. Such techniques employ a variety of analytic tools that enable researchers to make informed predictions and conclusions. Strength, weakness, opportunity, and threat analysis

21

(SWOT) and red team analysis will be used because of the complexity of the various international actors and the difficulty in identifying the intentions of each while maintaining an unbiased perspective. Link analysis will examine existing evidence of possible geopolitical agendas for each country involved by focusing on issues of narcotics trafficking, government response, and money laundering in the TBA and suggests areas for further study. Analysis of Competing Hypotheses (ACH) will explore possible alternatives of Chinese involvement in the TBA.

Through the structured planning method of SWOT analysis, specific objectives pertaining to Chinese interests in Latin America will be considered. SWOT analysis aids the policymaker in the decision-making process, helping them determine the best course of action. This technique provides both advantages and disadvantages. It will consider the potential for exploitation of developing countries and catalogs the risks associated when narco-terrorism becomes a potent force within the same. The particular purpose of SWOT in this study is to identify the internal and external factors China requires in order to achieve their desired end state.

Within the scope of this study, a unique challenge exists to understand the behaviors of foreign leaders or groups. Existing literature provides in-depth knowledge on how China perceives external threats and potential opportunities. How China views the U.S. is key in understanding the potential motivations behind China's increasing involvement in Latin America. Red team analysis will provide the perspective of the adversary, identifying ways in which China's rise in power and global status might influence Beijing's behavior in Latin America, more specifically the TBA.

Link analysis will examine relationships among transnational organized crime and terrorist groups operating in the TBA. This method of analysis can identify a narcotics trafficking nexus, for example. And most importantly, link analysis will be used to examine the relationship between China and Latin America. It will also provide visualization and theoretical examination of the aforementioned relationships between people, organizations, or events.

Analysis of competing hypotheses will be used to weigh alternative explanations and conclusions. The presence of both the Chinese government and Chinese-associated illegal activities in the TBA study presents a difficult intelligence issue, to wit: there may be several possible explanations for Chinese involvement in Latin America. ACH aids in the identification of reasonable alternatives and compares those alternatives concurrently. Evidence supporting competing hypotheses will be drawn from conditions conducive to narco-terrorism in the TBA and their correlations with China. Due to the difficulty of simultaneous evaluation, however, explanations will be limited to security and economic interests.

Following the identification of competing hypotheses, indicators that are anticipated for each explanation will be reviewed. This provides a baseline for tracking events and facilitates the identification of emerging trends. Indicators that will be considered are the Chinese government influence on legitimate and illicit economies in the TBA, the presence of narcotics trafficking in the TBA as well as the presence of terrorist organizations, the presence of transnational organized crime, and other pertinent geopolitical factors.

This chapter outlined the research methodology that will be used in this study. Structured analytic techniques such as SWOT Analysis, Red Team Analysis, Link Analysis, and Analysis of Competing Hypotheses (ACH) (Convergence, State-sponsored, and Unconnected) were chosen based on the facts and findings that are currently prevalent in the region and can be readily accessed for continued research for this study. The purpose of these techniques is to identify known associations, identify reasonable alternatives, and establish intent. The next chapter will review the data and analysis conducted for this study.

---

[1]U.S. Government, *A Tradecraft Primer: Structured Analytic Techniques for Improving Intelligence Analysis* (Washington, DC: Government Printing Office, March 2009), https://www.cia.gov/library/center-for-the-study-of-intelligence/csi-publications/ books-and-monographs/Tradecraft%20Primer-apr09.pdf (accessed May 15, 2013).

CHAPTER 4

ANALYSIS

The purpose of this research was to determine if relationships exist between the Chinese government, transnational organized crime, and terrorist organizations within the Tri-Border Area of South America and identify possible strategic implications of the same. The research question selected is: Does the Chinese government support narco-terrorism in the Tri-Border Area which poses a threat to U.S. security objectives in Latin America? The previous chapter outlined the various structured analytic techniques used in this study for the purpose of identifying intent, known associations, possible alternatives, and Chinese objectives in Latin America. This chapter will evaluate the strategic position of China; review how Chinese perceptions drive their actions; explore the relationships among terrorist organizations, transnational criminal organizations, and the corrupted officials that they exploit; and consider whether there is only a convergence of threats or a concerted Chinese effort to destabilize the region.

SWOT Analysis

Strengths, weaknesses, opportunities, and threats (SWOT) analysis is a technique for evaluating the strategic position of China or any other nation that might threaten U.S. security. This analysis enables the identification of internal and external factors that are advantageous or detrimental to the Chinese government in achieving its desired strategic objectives. Moreover, SWOT analysis provides key insight into the competitive advantage China may have in the development of emerging countries by identifying:

1. Strengths are those characteristics advantageous to China.

2. Weaknesses are those characteristics disadvantageous to China.

3. Opportunities are vulnerabilities that China could exploit to Beijing's advantage.

4. Threats are elements of the strategic environment that possess a significant risk to China.

Additionally, SWOT analysis will identify internal and external factors critical to achieving Chinese objectives by considering: (1) the strengths and weaknesses internal to China and (2) the opportunities and threats external to China. This analysis is critical in understanding the strategic environment in order to respond accordingly.

First, China's strength is directly tied to their economic growth, which has soared due to increasing investments in developing countries and high export rates. According to a 2011 Center for American Progress report, "China is now investing in many of the building blocks of innovation-driven economic growth that the United States has all but abandoned over the past decades."[1]

Second, China's weakness is endemic in its own labor forces and population–the risk of demands from labor and potential ethnic unrest. Economic forces are arguably raising wages. In order to maintain competiveness, however, the Chinese Communist Party (CCP) must maintain the status quo. Ethnic minorities in Tibet, Xinjiag, and Inner Mongolia threaten the general and ideological stability of the Chinese Communist regime.

Third, opportunities lie in exploiting American vulnerabilities. The recognition of potential "non-military war operations" as instruments of national power could have

26

increased significance in Chinese strategy. For instance, China has arguably employed "resource warfare" against the United States by unfairly subsidizing U.S. exports and withholding essential raw materials for the development of clean energy technologies.[2] Other opportunities may lie in the control of resources and energy in Latin America.

Finally, investing in developing countries has proved to be advantageous for China. These countries often have weak state institutions and governments that deter Western investors. Not so for the Chinese. This is evident in Latin America. According to the Associated Press in 2011, the Brazilian Trade Minister commented that Brazil's total trade with China was over US$77 billion.[3] Consequently, the United States fell to just over US$60 billion in bilateral trade.[4]

Should China's global ambitions come to fruition, foreign powers will resist. It is unlikely, that the U.S. will want to take a backseat to any other nation. In anticipation of possible coming world changes, bilateral defense relationships are already becoming more prevalent. Political responses to China's rise have so far included: strategic dialogue between India and Japan focusing on intelligence cooperation, Japanese support to Vietnam's maritime forces, and a closer Japanese-Australian strategic partnership.[5] Furthermore, the United State's strategic rebalance to Asia-Pacific has reaffirmed U.S. commitments in the region. However, China requires access to markets and recourses in order for China to maintain economic growth.

In summary, it is essential that China maintains economic growth in order to ensure stability at home. To do so, China must engage countries that offer access to markets and natural recourses. With increased investments also brings a level of influence, which can be leveraged in order to counter foreign pressures. The next section will examine the perspective of China through red team analysis.

Red Team Analysis

How China views the U.S. is key in understanding the potential motives for Chinese involvement in Latin America. Red team analysis is typically used at the onset of the decision-making process in order to ensure the information is viewed through the lens of China. Utilizing the four ways of seeing provides that perspective and examines how Beijing views the United States.

Beijing assumes that as China rises, the United States will resist that rise and China will be seen as a possible threat to U.S. predominance.[6] Chinese foreign policy is defensive–"to blunt destabilizing influences from abroad, to avoid territorial losses, to reduce its neighbors' suspicions, and to sustain economic growth."[7] Moreover, China desires a global role that serves its economic interests.

The Chinese believe that the United States is attempting to restrain Beijing's "political influence and harm Chinese interests."[8] "Over the past several years, it has been common practice for Chinese academics and pundits to describe the U.S. 'pivot' or 'rebalancing' to Asia as part of a greater strategy of containment."[9] Conversely, "many in Washington insist that the relationship with China is one of engagement and is highly successful in a number of spheres, including trade, counter-proliferation, and global governance."[10]

Beijing perceives the United States as duplicitous. The U.S.-China Strategic and Economic Dialogue supports cooperation. However, Washington openly criticizes China on territorial security concerns with adjacent countries as well as internal security

28

concerns with ethnic unrest. U.S. presence is felt in all of these concerns. For the Chinese, Taiwan continues to be a "sensitive issue in U.S.-China relations."[11] "The Obama administration's decision to sell US$5.8 billion in arms to Taiwan has been roundly criticized by Beijing."[12] To Beijing, arms sells "pose a terrible threat to the Peoples Republic of China."[13] China believes that its "political stability and territorial integrity are threatened by foreign actors and forces."[14]

China's large population make it necessary to secure sources of commodities, such as petroleum, gain access to markets and investments, and to recruit allies for China's positions on international norms and legal regimes.[15] However, while the Chinese invest in developing countries, China "does not seek local political control," only influence.[16] China seeks "sustained long-term demand for commodities" and will "aggressively work the diplomacy on a bilateral basis."[17]

From the U.S. point of view, China is expansionistic and assertive. Over the past decade, "China has increased its military spending by an average of more than 10 percent per year as it seeks to modernize its defense forces."[18] China is steadily increasing its capability of force projection within the South China Sea.[19] Additionally, China is opportunistic and will act on perceived advantages in the current global system. Continued economic growth is essential to Beijing's geopolitical imperatives. That is, China will seek strategic partnerships that offer access to natural recourses and markets allowing China to maintain its economic growth.

Future trends seem to suggest that "even if China becomes the world's largest economy, its prosperity and the world's prosperity will remain dependent on the economies of global rivals U.S. and Japan."[20] The U.S. and the demands of China's own population will manage China's rise. Furthermore, "healthcare, environmental costs" and a "rising dependence on foreign energy and food" will inherently slow China's rise.[21]

The Four Ways of Seeing depicted in figure 2 illustrates that the United States perceives China as expansionistic and assertive based on increased economic investments in developing countries and increased military capabilities. Conversely, China perceives the United States as duplicitous and interfering in internal affairs due to incompatibility between strategic communications and actions. China views itself as the natural leader in Asia, which should be regarded as an equal to the United States. However, the U.S. views itself as the preeminent power. Perceptions aside, Chinese national interests may compete with or even oppose U.S. national interests.

How US Views Itself
- Preeminent Power

How US Views PRC
- Expansionist
- Assertive

How PRC Views US
- Threat to Political Stability and Territorial Integrity
- Duplicitous

How PRC Views Itself
- Natural Leader in Asia

Figure 2.   Four Ways of Seeing

Source: Created by author.

In summary, there are clear differences between how the United States and China are perceived by the other. This is possibly due to the level of uncertainty that exists concerning the outcome of China's rise. Nevertheless, globalization has interconnected the United States and China. As for Latin America, China will continue to seek access to markets and recourses. This section provided a basic understanding of the potential motives for Chinese involvement in Latin America, assuming that Chinese global perceptions are the same as Chinese-Latin American perceptions. The next section will identify criminal links between China and Latin America as well as links between transnational organized crime and terrorism in order to determine the relationship between these aforementioned groups.

Link Analysis

Link analysis will evaluate the relationships between terrorist organizations, transnational criminal organizations, and local commercial or governmental groups operating in the TBA. Additionally, possible criminal ties between China and Latin America will be explored. The purpose of link analysis is to identify patterns and trends.

Links between narcotics traffickers and terrorist organizations have been well documented over the past several years as terrorist groups have increasingly turned to drug trafficking as a source of revenue.[22] The link between transnational organized crime and terrorist organizations is one of shared means and collaboration. According to the Federal Research Division in 2002, "About half of the 28 groups officially designated as terrorist organizations by the U.S. Department of State are believed to have ties to drug trafficking."[23]

Multiple Islamic terrorist groups share a presence in the TBA. These groups include Hizballah and, to a lesser extent, Sunni extremist groups.[24] "Argentina's Secretary of Intelligence (SI)" assessed that Luis Fernando de Costa, who facilitated "several Russian arms shipments to Colombia's FARC," is associated with several "Lebanese businessmen affiliated or sympathizers to Hizballah."[25] Whereas, Hizballah is known to conduct narcotics trafficking from Latin America into Europe and the Middle East using the cities of Foz do Iguacu and Ciudad del Este as "transit points for smuggling Columbian cocaine."[26] The arrest of a Lebanese citizen by the Brazilian Federal Police in January 2003 "exposed an operation that was moving between 400 and 1,000 kilos of Colombian cocaine per month via Foz do Iguacu."[27] Moreover, the distinction between "Islamist-related militant activity" and legitimate businessmen is arduous due to the level of financial support that the ethnic Lebanese community provides to "Shiite organizations as Hizballah and Amal."[28]

In addition to terrorist groups, "the TBA provides a haven that is geographically, socially, economically, and politically highly conducive for allowing organized crime and the corrupt officials who accept their bribes or payoffs to operate in a symbiotic relationship that thrives on drug and arms trafficking, money laundering, and other lucrative criminal activities."[29] Chinese transnational organized crime has direct ties with Islamic terrorist groups in the TBA. The Chinese mafia is known to "collaborate with the Islamic terrorist groups in the region."[30] "The convergence among Chinese triads and terrorist organizations is not limited to Hizballah, because the regional intelligence services admit that they also work with the Egyptian al-Gama Islamiyya (Islamic Group), among others."[31] The Sung-I family shipped munitions to the Egyptian al-Gama's al-

Islamiyya, which was intercepted in Cyprus.[32] Furthermore, the Ming family managed the Egyptian terrorist group's funds from within the TBA.[33] Another example of collaboration is one of trafficking of contraband. "Reportedly, the Hong Kong Mafia engages in large-scale trafficking in pirated products from mainland China to Ciudad del Este and Hong Kong-based crime groups maintain strong ties with the pro-Iranian Hizballah in the TBA."[34]

Associations can also be found between transnational organized crime and corrupt business executives, politicians, and military officers in the TBA as well as in the affected countries.[35] This is evident in the testimony of a former Iranian intelligence officer in the aftermath of the 1994 bombing at Buenos Aires's Ezeiza International Airport. The witness testified "the Iranian government organized and carried out the attack and then paid then-president Carlos Saul Menem US$10 million to cover it up."[36] However, the charges were unsubstantiated. The Argentine Ministry of Public Health of Misiones Province reported associations between the Civil Police of Foz do Iguacu and narcotics networks within the TBA as early as 2000, which resulted in the suspension of the officers involved.[37] More recently, in June 2010, a Brazilian Secretary of Justice, Romeu Tuma Junior, was dismissed for his alleged associations with the Chinese mafia.[38]

The link between the Chinese government and Chinese corporations may not be obvious for those more familiar with capitalism. As a Communist state, the Chinese government practices state-ownership of business entities known as government-owned corporations. These government-owned corporations may be partially or fully owned and operated by the Chinese government. This concept dates back to 1949 when all businesses were established and owned by the government. Following economic reforms in the 1990s the Chinese government accepted privatization–reducing state-ownership from over 100,000 to around 20,000 companies.[39]

However, the inverse is true for companies deemed strategic. The Chinese government has taken initiatives to strengthen government authority over strategic state-owned enterprises.[40] The industries that are considered as strategic are "defense, power generation and distribution, oil and petrochemicals, telecommunications, coal, aviation, and shipping."[41] Corporate executives are often appointed by the Chinese Communist Party and are perceived as government officials. "Their power and influence–particularly their links to the ruling Communist Party and government–give partners and competitors pause."[42] Chinese state-owned oil companies are seeking additional investment opportunities in Argentina and Brazil. But with increased investments bring an influx of Chinese transnational criminal organizations.

These same associations are also present in Africa where Chinese organized crime syndicates have been operating in the sub-Sahara since the 1970s.[43]

> The recent emergence of China as a major diplomatic and business operator in Africa, and the arrival in the continent of substantial numbers of Chinese expatriates and even settlers, adds a further element to this chemistry. Chinese crime gangs have a long history in Africa. Their enhanced presence in the continent can be expected to result in collaboration with African interests, and the development of new illicit markets in China itself.[44]

"As organized crime and terrorist groups have globalized and diversified their operations in the past decade, they have based their activities in countries offering conditions most favorable to survival and expansion."[45] Additionally, other factors were found to be common among countries where transnational organized crime and terrorist activities persist. These affected countries exhibit poor economic conditions; weak state institutions, and a heterogeneous population.

For the sake of comparison, a U.S. Government report issued in December 2000 describes the conditions in Africa that support the presence of transnational organized crime and terrorist organizations as follows:

> Porous borders, ample routs for smuggling drugs, weapons, explosives, and other contraband, and corruptible police and security forces make Sub-Saharan Africa an inviting operational environment for international criminals, drug traffickers, and terrorists. Major Sub-Saharan cities with extensive commercial, financial, and sea and air transportation links to Europe, the Middle East, and Asia are hubs for international criminal activity. . . . These include Nairobi and Mombasa in Kenya, Addis Ababa in Ethiopia, Abidjan in Cote d'Ivoire, Johannesburg in South Africa, and Lagos in Nigeria.[46]

The Chinese has increased economic initiatives in developing countries. These countries often have poor economies conditions that allow China to gain access to those markets. Additionally, these countries have weak institutions and are prone to corruption. Both can be leveraged in order to ensure Chinese interests are met. Furthermore, Chinese transnational criminal organizations emerge in areas of Chinese investments. These indicators are observed in both Latin America and Africa developing a pattern of associations.

A link diagram, figure 3, depicts direct associations between transnational criminal organizations and terrorist organizations operating in the TBA based on the evidence provided. Additionally, direct associations persist between transnational criminal organizations and local officials. However, suspected links exist between terrorist organizations and local officials. Associations are only suspected between transnational criminal organizations and Chinese government-owned companies operating in Latin America. The link diagram does illustrate a high degree of network density, indicating complex levels of coordination among various criminal, terrorist and governmental groups in the TBA.

35

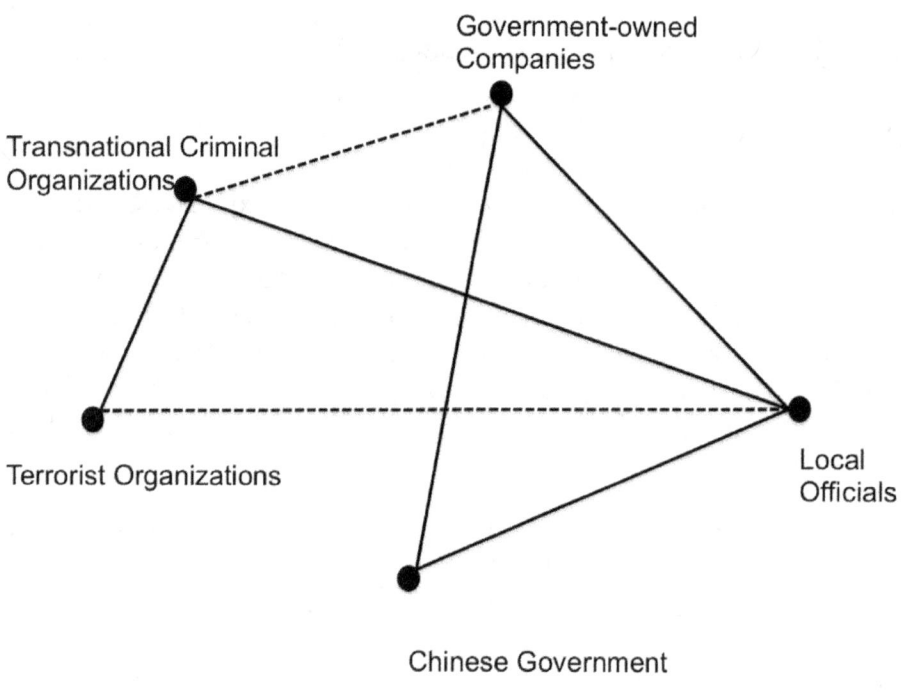

Figure 3.   Link Diagram

Source: Created by author.

Transnational criminal organizations are in the same spectrum of terrorist organizations, but reside at opposite ends of that spectrum. Each move through the spectrum depending on their respective objectives, political or economic, and methods employed in achieving those desired objectives, often the activities of both overlap in the middle of the spectrum. Furthermore, given an increase of decentralization among terrorist organizations, a natural evolution is likely that resembles that of transnational organized crime. This is evident in the recent fragmentation of al Qaeda. Without centralized leadership and funding, al Qaeda franchises are turning to criminal activities for fundraising and their objectives are shifting away from purely political ends. In doing so, collaboration with traditional transnational criminal organizations and the inherent criminal links between origin, and host countries will become more problematic especially in states susceptible to corruption.

In summary, clear associations exist between terrorist organizations and transnational criminal organizations. This is evident in the collaboration between Chinese mafias and Hizballah and Hamas operating in the TBA. Both are linked to narco-trafficking. Additionally, these drug trafficking organizations have suspected links to business as well as government officials due to corruption. Chinese transnational criminal organizations create an inherent criminal link between China and Latin America. Moreover, global trends indicate with increased Chinese economic initiatives, an increase in Chinese transnational organized crime is observed. The next section will examine possible hypotheses as to the scope of China's involvement is in the TBA.

Analysis of Competing Hypotheses (ACH)

There may be several possible explanations for the proliferation of Chinese interests in Latin America. In order to gain an understanding of Chinese involvement, three competing hypotheses of convergence, state-sponsored, and unconnected bear examination. The first competing hypothesis is convergence, which is a combination of Chinese transnational organized crime, terrorism, and Chinese interests based on the current conditions of the TBA. The second competing hypothesis is state-sponsored, which the Chinese government conducts non-military war operations to include narco-trafficking in order to shape the future security environment. The third competing hypothesis is unconnected, which the illicit and illegal operations that occur in the TBA are isolated and unrelated to Chinese involvement whereas China's role is limited to legitimate economic interests.

Convergence

The first competing hypothesis addresses the convergence of Chinese transnational criminal organizations, terrorist organizations, and Chinese economic interests in the TBA. A combination of motives–money, tactics, geography, and politics–weave together terrorist networks and transnational organized crime groups to the advantage of each. Terrorist organizations for which the ends justifies the means often engage in criminal activities–illicit trafficking, money laundering, and corruption in order to obtain the financial recourses to carry out their agendas. Their alliances with transnational organized crime syndicates are usually volatile; shared ideology is rarely an issue. The most important thing is the maintenance of a steady cash flow. Beyond this basic purpose, separate terrorist groups and syndicates are welcome to pursue correlative goals–to accrue political power in a region, to challenge the superpower status of the West, to exact justice or revenge upon one's enemies, or to wage holy war. Because transnational organized crime share terroristic methods, such as violence directed toward local officials, it can become difficult to separate the terrorists from the criminals and nearly impossible to launch an effective opposition to either.[47]

The porous borders, existing smuggling routes, weak state institutions, and corruption make the TBA a haven for Islamic terrorist groups to carry out their activities unhindered. These activities "include fund-raising and proselytizing among the zone's Middle Eastern population, as well as document forging, money laundering, contraband smuggling, and weapons and drug trafficking."[48] Narcotics trafficking is a major activity of Hizballah networks within the TBA.[49] The U.S. Department of State in 2002 assessed that the TBA is a significant transit corridor for trafficking Andean cocaine to the

38

Atlantic coast of Brazil.[50] These same environmental conditions also support transnational criminal organizations.

Criminal ties between the People's Republic of China (PRC) and Latin America are becoming amplified resulting from the increased interaction of the two regions.[51] With this increase of Chinese investment, Chinese mafias establish a presence and operate within the Chinese communities. Due to the closed nature of the Chinese community in the TBA, reporting to local officials is limited.[52] However, "Chinese mafias have a recognized presence" in the TBA since the 1990s and have ties to mainland China.[53] Additionally, reporting on extortion targeting local Chinese business has increased in news media outlets across Argentina.

The hypothesis of "convergence" does not fully explain the China-Latin America criminal ties. The emergence of Chinese transnational organized crime in areas of overseas Chinese investment possibly is the result of opportunistic criminal activity. However, corrupt executives within government-owned companies could also leverage transnational organized crime in order to further corporate interests. Corruption may be a key factor in the criminal links between China and Latin America. After all, the Chinese Communist Party recognizes corruption as a current threat to Chinese institutions. In a recent public address, President Xi Jinping stated that countering corruption is a priority as it is a threat to the Communist Party. If corruption is the cause of suspected links between Chinese government-owned companies then evidence should support this argument. However, there is clearly a lack of evidence that either corroborates or absolves the Chinese government's involvement.

State-sponsored

The second competing hypothesis posits state-sponsorship where the Chinese government is conducting narcotics trafficking operations in the TBA. "According to Sergio Cesarin, a well-known Argentine-China scholar, when looking at China's role in Latin America, one should consider China's aspirations to increase its influence in the international system through the construction of political, economic, and military power."[54] The Chinese have progressively inserted themselves in Latin America. "China is seen as an opportunity for Latin America to break the existing North-South asymmetry, forging friendships among neighboring countries."[55]

The permissive nature of the TBA offers China the ability to apply a combination of "non-military war operations" directed toward the United States. In order to overcome the technological advantage of the U.S. "the doctrine of total war outlined in *Unrestricted Warfare* clearly demonstrates the People's Republic of China is prepared to confront the United States and our allies by conducting 'asymmetrical' or multidimensional attacks on almost every aspect of our social, economical, and political life."[56]

As argued by Douglass and Stanton, the Chinese government uses drugs as a weapon of subversion directed toward the United States. Opium and precursor chemicals are trafficked from Asia, through West Africa, and into Brazil destined for markets in the United States. Through the use of narco-terrorism, China could destabilize the region in order to shift American recourses away from the Pacific–limiting U.S. interference in Chinese geopolitical goals.

Mao, the father of modern China, perceived both internal and external challenges to his nation. He sought a continuous revolution at home and a long-term objective of challenging the current international order.[57]

> Long Live the Victory of People's War, a 1965 pamphlet by Lin Biao, then Mao's presumptive successor, argued that the countryside of the world (that is, the developing countries) would defeat the cities of the world (that is, the advanced countries) much as the People's Liberation Army (PLA) had defeated Chiang Kai-shek.[58]

Chinese support of narco-terrorism in the TBA may be fundamental to this ideology. China can influence the future security environment by hastening American decline. "Debate about the future role of the U.S. in Latin America concerns not only the decline of U.S. capability, but also how other nations may affect U.S. policy."[59] China believes its increasing influence in developing countries can be leveraged to affect U.S. policy and ultimately diminish U.S. hegemony in the western hemisphere.

However, this hypothesis does not consider that China's objectives may have changed. Douglass and Stanton claim that Mao Tse-tung developed a strategy of utilizing opium as a weapon targeted against the Communist opposition and later as a weapon of subversion to use against the West in order to finance clandestine activities, moral and physical weakening of opposing populations, and the destruction of the will of U.S. servicemen in Vietnam.[60] These objectives would have been realized in the 1970s. Furthermore, it is highly unlikely that China would support such activities given the economic interests with suspected targeted countries. If Chinese government involvement was recognized, China would lose access to markets and natural resources. Furthermore, no evidence of Chinese government drug trafficking operations was uncovered contrary to claims in *Red Cocaine*.

41

Unconnected

The third competing hypothesis posits that the illicit and illegal operations that occur in the TBA are unconnected to Chinese involvement pertaining to economic interests in the region. China is driven by necessity as well as political ambition. "China has an increasing demand for resources and energy, some of which have to be imported from abroad."[61] This growing demand is evident in China's mercantilist ambitions in developing countries. These countries receive needed investments that translate into infrastructure and China maintains its ability to meet global demand for consumer goods. China also has seen an increase in sales of military goods to these developing countries.

"Latin American markets are becoming increasingly valuable for Chinese companies because they allow the PRC to expand and diversify its export base at a time when economic growth is slowing in traditional markets such as the United States and Europe."[62] Some local interests do exist in such countries as Brazil and Argentina, however, that resist China's resource grab, but their resistance may be short-lived.[63] China's increasing demand for resources and energy make overcoming this resistance necessary.[64]

China's perception is that the United States is attempting to contain Beijing's global agenda. Through economic power, China can increase its influence in the international system.[65] For the Chinese, the current security environment is in transition, resulting in "a division of spheres of influence."[66] Beijing desires multipolarity with five poles, which will eventually give China the economic hegemony it desires. "Once economic hegemony is achieved, political and military hegemony will follow."[67] China is increasing its influence in developing countries that can be leveraged to affect U.S. policy and ultimately diminish U.S. hegemony in the western hemisphere.

Again, counter arguments can be made in an attempt to disprove this hypothesis. First, China-Latin America criminal ties do exist and are not considered. Secondly, Latin American countries offer China access to markets and recourses and in return investments. Finally, arguments can be made that "a pluralistic world structure one superpower and four powers already exists."[68]

ACH Discussion

Table 1 depicts a matrix with the three competing hypotheses across the top with evidence on the side. E1 considers China-Latin American criminal ties, which is evidence of Chinese transnational criminal organizations conduct operations in both China and the TBA. E2 reflects evidence of Chinese economic interests in the region. E3 indicates evidence of narcotics trafficking in the TBA. E4 is evidence that the conditions in the TBA support both illegal operations and legitimate trade. The evidence was considered as being consistent (C), inconsistent (I), or neutral (N) to each hypothesis. Additionally, this technique focuses on disproving a hypothesis, not proving one. This clearly illustrates that some of the evidence is consistent with multiple hypotheses and becomes less valuable in disproving the hypothesis.

Chinese transnational criminal organizations collaborate with Islamic terrorist organizations in the TBA and share similar methods, all of which centers around narco-trafficking. Increased Chinese investment in Latin America also provides additional opportunities for Chinese transnational criminal organizations to exploit the local ethnic Chinese communities in the TBA. Again, it is unlikely that the Chinese government

43

would jeopardize access to markets and natural recourses in order to conduct non-military war operations directed towards the United States. Moreover, the existing conditions in the TBA support transnational organized crime, terrorism, and Chinese economic initiatives. With that said, the evidence supports convergence. Evidence of China-Latin America criminal ties is consistent with both "convergence" and "state-sponsored" hypotheses. Evidence of economic interests is consistent with both "convergence" and "unrelated" hypotheses. The evidence of narcotics trafficking was only consistent with the "convergence" hypothesis. The existing conditions of weak institutions, a government prone to corruption, and a vulnerable economy referred to as "operational environment" is consistent with all hypotheses.

	Table 1. ACH			
	Weight	H1	H2	H3
		Convergence	State-Sponsored	Unrelated
E1	China-Latin America Criminal Ties	C	C	I
E2	Economic Interests	C	I	C
E3	Narcotics Trafficking	C	I	I
E4	Operational Environment	C	C	C

Source: Created by author.

In summary, evidence clearly supports the competing hypothesis of convergence. Latin America offers the same operational environment conducive for China's economic growth and the terrorist-transnational organized crime spectrum. Moreover, the China-

Latin America criminal ties are compounded due to increased interaction. The next section will assist in determining conclusions and recommendations.

The primary question for this thesis was "Does the Chinese government support narco-terrorism in the Tri-Border Area which poses a threat to U.S. security objectives in Latin America?" Based on the data presentation and analysis from this chapter, the answer is no–narco-terrorism poses a threat to U.S. security objectives in the TBA, but there is insufficient evidence that this is directly supported by the Chinese government. China's involvement in Latin America is based on availability of markets and access to recourses required to maintain economic growth. As a result of increased investments in Latin America, China gain influence in the region that could be leveraged in order to offset foreign pressures. Chinese investments in developing countries can be perceived as assertive, whereas, China's rise creates uncertainty in the strategic environment. Nevertheless, clear links persist between Chinese transnational criminal organizations, terrorist organizations, and the corrupt officials they exploit. These relationships create an inherent China-Latin America criminal link that is compounded due to increased interaction. Finally, evidence supports the hypothesis of convergence due to the existing conditions that are conducive for both narco-terrorism and Chinese economic interests. The next chapter will discuss conclusions and the implications for the United States and Latin America.

---

[1]Kate Gordon, Susan Lyon, Ed Paisley, and Sean Pool, "Rising to the Challenge: A Progressive U.S. Approach to China's Innovation and Competitiveness Policies," www.americanprogress.org/issues/2011/01/pdf/china_innovation.pdf (accessed May 15, 2013) 2.

[2]Ibid., 1.

[3]Ana Cristina Alves, "China's Resource Quest in Brazil: The Changing Role of Economic Statecraft," *Portuguese Journal of International Affairs*, no. 6 (Spring/Summer 2011): 30.

[4]Ibid.

[5]Luttwak, 96.

[6]Andrew J. Nathan and Andrew Scobell, "How China Sees America," *Foreign Affairs* (August 25, 2012): 32-35.

[7]Ibid., 32.

[8]Ibid., 35.

[9]John Hemmings, "Hedging: The Real U.S. Policy towards China," *The Diplomat*, http://thediplomat.com/the-editor/2013/05/13/hedging-the-real-u-s-policy-towards-china/ (accessed May 27, 2013).

[10]Ibid.

[11]Cui Tiankai and Pang Hanzhao, "China-U.S. Relations in China's Overall Diplomacy in the New Era," http://www.fmprc.gov.cn/eng/zxxx/t953682.htm (accessed May 27, 2013).

[12]Wenran Jiang, "The Danger for U.S..-China Ties," *The Diplomat*, http://thediplomat.com/2011/10/01/the-danger-for-us-china-ties/ (accessed May 27, 2013).

[13]Cui and Pang.

[14]Nathan and Scobell, 35.

[15]Ibid., 34.

[16]Barnett.

[17]Ibid.

[18]Michael Swaine, "Avoiding U.S.-China Military Rivalry," *The Diplomat*, http://thediplomat.com/whats-next-china/avoiding-us-china-military-rivalry/ (accessed May 27, 2013).

[19]Ibid.

[20]Nathan and Scobell, 46.

[21]Barnett.

[22]Berry et al., 2.

[23]Ibid., 3.

[24]Ibid., 14.

[25]Horacio Calderon, "Organized Crime and Terrorism in the Triple Border Area," *Buenos Aires* (August 24, 2007), 5.

[26]Hudson, 42.

[27]Ibid., 26.

[28]Calderon, 7.

[29]Berry et al., 3.

[30]Hudson, 42.

[31]Calderon, 7.

[32]Hudson, 42.

[33]Ibid., 43.

[34]Ibid.

[35]Berry et al., 184.

[36]Hudson, 47.

[37]Ibid., 63.

[38]Ellis, "Chinese Organized Crime in Latin America," 66-75.

[39]Forbes, "What Capitalists Should Know About State-Owned Enterprises," http://www.forbes.com/sites/hbsworkingknowledge/2013/02/22/what-capitalists-should-know-about-state-owned-enterprises/ (accessed May 15, 2013).

[40]Mikael Mattlin, "Chinese Strategic State-Owned Enterprises and Ownership Control," http://www.vub.ac.be/biccs/site/assets/files/apapers/Asia%20papers/Asia%20Paper%204(6).pdf (accessed May 15, 2013), 23.

[41]Ibid., 13.

[42]Jonathan R. Woetzel, "Reassessing China's State-Owned Enterprises," http://www.mckinseyquarterly.com/Reassessing_Chinas_state_owned_enterprises_2149 (accessed May 15, 2013).

[43]Stephen Ellis, "West Africa's International Drug Trade," http://users.polisci. wisc.edu/schatzberg/ps363/Ellis2009.pdf (accessed May 15, 2013).

[44]Ibid.

[45]Berry et al., 1.

[46]International Crime Threat Assessment, www.fas.org/irp/threat/pub45270 chap3.html (accessed May 15, 2013).

[47]Hudson, 32.

[48]Ibid., 14.

[49]Ibid., 24.

[50]Ibid.

[51]Ellis, "Chinese Organized Crime in Latin America," 66-75.

[52]Ibid.

[53]Ibid.

[54]Hulse, 38.

[55]Ibid.

[56]Col. Qiao Liang and Col. Wang Xiangsui, *Unrestricted Warfare* (Panama City, Panama: Pan American Publishing Company, 2002), x.

[57]Henry Kissinger, *On China* (New York: Penguin Books, 2011), 99.

[58]Ibid., 105.

[59]Michael Pillsbury, *China Debates the Future Security Environment* (Honolulu: University Press of the Pacific), 311.

[60]Douglass, 11.

[61]Edward Luttwak, *The Rise of China vs. the Logic of Strategy* (Cambridge, MA: The Belknap Press of Harvard University Press, 2012), 70.

[62]Ellis, "Chinese Soft Power in Latin America," 85-90.

[63]Ibid.

[64]Luttwak, 70.

[65]Hulse, 38.

[66]Pillsbury, 308

[67]Ibid., 310.

[68]Ibid., 311.

CHAPTER 5

CONCLUSIONS AND RECOMMENDATIONS

The purpose of this research was to determine if relationships exist between the Chinese government, transnational organized crime, and terrorist organizations within the Tri-Border Area of South America and identify possible strategic implications of the same. The research question selected is: Does the Chinese government support narco-terrorism in the Tri-Border Area, which poses a threat to U.S. security objectives in Latin America? The previous chapter reviewed findings and analysis, concluding that the answer was no–narco-terrorism poses a threat to U.S. security objectives in the TBA, but there is insufficient evidence that this is directly supported by the Chinese government. This chapter will provide the conclusions of this study and suggest recommendations.

Conclusions

The research conducted in support of this study suggests that a convergence of transnational organized crime, terrorist organizations, and corruption forms the nexus that supports narco-terrorism in the TBA. Evidence does not implicate the Chinese government in supporting transnational organized crime, terrorist organizations, or narco-trafficking. Additionally, it is highly unlikely that China would support such activities given the economic interests within the region and with the United States. However, further research into the activities of Chinese crime syndicates operating in the TBA is warranted considering the density of those networks, Beijing's view of the West, and China's ambition of pursuing the role of the largest global superpower. Nevertheless, the convergence of security threats in the TBA, compounded by an increased Chinese presence, has strategic implications for both Latin America and the United States.

In Latin America's developing nations, clear links persist between transnational organized crime and terrorist networks. Suspected links exist between the aforementioned groups and corrupt officials in both government-owned companies and local governments. The degree of density of these relationships indicates a high level of coordination among groups involved in black trade, i.e., narcotics trafficking, piracy, etc. Disparate groups operating in the TBA at present may have dissimilar ideological objectives, but cooperation exits among them nonetheless.

The U.S. focus on persistent conflict in Iraq and Afghanistan, the threat of nuclear proliferation in North Korea and Iran, and the domestic debt crisis has resulted in limited American response in countering the threat that narco-terrorism represented in the TBA. U.S. capacity-building efforts in Latin America have waivered over the past decade. Strengthening state institutions and building security force capabilities in the TBA would enable a more effective response in order to counter narco-terrorism in the region as well as in the United States. Moreover, regional governments have limited means to counter the growing challenge of increasing criminal ties between Latin America and China.

An effort has been made by the security forces of Argentina, Brazil, and Paraguay in order to counter transnational organized crime and terrorism. However, multiple factors inhibit the effectiveness of security forces in the region. The lack of capabilities and resources are only exacerbated by the inadequate legal systems and corruption. In Argentina, laws do exist for narcotics related activities, but do not "define organized crime legally."[1] The Brazilian government "has been generally dismissive of reports of terrorists operating in the area."[2] As for Paraguay, Ciudad del Este's police force consists of only 200 personnel and "is suspected of corruption."[3]

With expanding Chinese investments in Latin America, criminal activities between these two regions are likely to increase as well. Regional law enforcement agencies have "not made a significant effort to penetrate the Chinese communities in their jurisdictions, all too often allowing what happens in the Chinese barrios to be the business of the communities themselves."[4] This gap creates the opportunity for transnational organized crime to expand their operations.

Transnational organized crime and terrorist organizations have exploited the U.S. absence in the TBA. With that said, the emergence of criminal ties between China and Latin America affect the U.S. in several ways. First, the TBA is an active drug trafficking corridor where opiates and precursor chemicals are destined for the U.S.[5] Second, transnational organized crime elements that are targeted by the U.S. often utilize Chinese banks for money laundering operations.[6] Furthermore, these activities have a destabilizing effect on the countries involved. Finally, the presence of Chinese influence further complicates an already dynamic security environment.

Terrorism is evolving into transnational organized crime, non-state actors are influencing foreign policy, and state actors are seeking to further their own, often competing, strategic interests. Moreover, the convergence of these threats combined with competing foreign interests threatens our national security in ways we could not have imagined a decade ago. "The United States has a strategic interest in working with both the PRC and Latin American governments to manage the challenge posed by expanding China-Latin America criminal ties."[7]

A multilateral approach may be necessary to counter these emerging threats within the TBA, which involves China. The U.S. has an opportunity to reaffirm commitments in Latin America while developing a dialogue with Beijing in order to combat this transnational threat. The United States is no longer the sole power with interests in Latin America. As a result, the inclusion of China is necessary to address China-Latin America criminal ties due to potential political ramifications. "Collaboration on organized crime among the United States, China, and the countries of Latin America could be an important vehicle for building confidence and overcoming tension as China expands its presence in Latin America in the context of the dominant U.S. position there."[8]

Recommendations

Based on the findings of this research, there are a number of recommendations for policy makers that follow. These are:

1. The United States must change its perception of terrorist organizations and view them for what they are–transnational criminal organizations. In doing so, capabilities and resources allocated to counter-terrorism cam be leveraged in order to effectively counter security threats posed by transnational organized crime.

2. Terrorist threats, economic instability, global trafficking in narcotics, people, and weapons are inherently inter-agency tasks. As U.S. national security strategy evolves to counter these ever-increasing threats, the United States must strengthen the inter-agency process in order to effectively conduct cross-agency operations. It is crucial that we respond, rather than react to these threats.

3. Due to the increased Chinese presence in Latin America, it is in the interest of the United States to include China in solving the challenges inherent to China-Latin America criminal ties.[9] The United States has an opportunity to establish a trilateral agreement showing not only commitment but also intent for U.S. interests in Latin America.

GEN (Ret) Wesley Clark addressed the issue of linkage of failed states and terrorism in 2004:

> Serious research and development efforts are required to produce technologies, strategies, organizations, and trained personnel who can go into failed states, work with our allies and friends, and promote the political and economic reforms that will meet popular needs and reduce the sources of terrorism and conflict.[10]

---

[1]Hudson, 62.

[2]Ibid., 64.

[3]Ibid., 65.

[4]Ellis, "Chinese Organized Crime in Latin America," 66-75.

[5]Ibid.

[6]Ibid.

[7]Ibid.

[8]Ibid.

[9]Ibid.

[10]Wesley Clark, *Winning Modern Wars* (New York: Public Affairs, 2004), 194.

BIBLIOGRAPHY

Books

Berry, LaVerle, Glen E. Curtis, John N. Gibbs, Rex Hudson, Tara Karacam, Nina Kollars, and Ramon Miro. *Nations Hospitable to Organized Crime and Terrorism*. Washington, DC: Library of Congress, 2003.

Candlin, A. H. Stanton. *Psycho-Chemical Warfare: The Chinese Communist Drug Offensive Against the West*. New Rochelle, NY: Arlington House, 1973.

Clark, Wesley. *Winning Modern Wars*. New York: Public Affairs, 2004.

Douglass, Joseph D. *Red Cocaine: The Drugging of America and the West*. New York: Edward Harle, 1999.

Hudson, Rex. *Terrorist and Organized Crime Groups in the Tri-Border Area (TBA) of South America*. Washington, DC: Library of Congress, 2003.

Kissinger, Henry. *On China*. New York: Penguin Books, 2011.

Liang, Qiao, and Wang Xiangsui. *Unrestricted Warfare: China's Master Plan to Destroy America*. Panama City, Panama: Pan American Publishing Company, 2002.

Luttwak, Edward. *The Rise of China vs. the Logic of Strategy*. Cambridge, MA: The Belknap Press of Harvard University Press, 2012.

Pillsbury, Michael. *China Debates the Future Security Environment*. Honolulu: University Press of the Pacific, 2005.

Tzu, Sun. *The Art of War*. Translated by Thomas Cleary. Boston: Shambhala, 1988.

UNODC. *World Drug Report 2012*. United Nations publication: Sales No. E.12.XI.1, 2012.

Periodicals

Alves, Ana Cristina. "China's Resource Quest in Brazil: The Changing Role of Economic Statecraft." *Portuguese Journal of International* Affairs, no. 6 (2011): 30-31

Ellis, R. Evan. "Chinese Organized Crime in Latin America." *PRISM* 4, no. 1 (2012): 66-75.

Ellis, R. Evan. "Chinese Soft Power in Latin America." *Joint Force Quarterly*, no. 60 (January 2011): 85-91.

Nathan, Andrew J., and Andrew Scobell. "How China Sees America." *Foreign Affairs* 91, no. 5 (October 2012): 32-35

Government Documents

U.S. Government. *A Tradecraft Primer: Structured Analytic Techniques for Improving Intelligence Analysis.* Washington, DC: CIA, March 2009. https://www.cia.gov/library/center-for-the-study-of-intelligence/csi-publications/books-and-monographs/Tradecraft%20Primer-apr09.pdf (accessed May 15, 2013).

U.S. Army. Command and General Staff College. *Master of Military Art and Science (MMAS) Research and Thesis.* Ft. Leavenworth, KS: USA CGSC, July 2003.

The White House. *2010 National Security Strategy.* Washington DC: The White House, May 2010.

———. *2011 National Drug Control Strategy.* Washington DC: The White House, 2011.

Research Project

Anderson, Wesley J. L. "Disrupting Threat Finances: Utilization of Financial Information to Disrupt Terrorist Organizations in the Twenty-First Century." Command and General Staff College, Fort Leavenworth, KS, April 2007.

Farah, Douglas. "Transnational Organized Crime, Terrorism, and Criminalized States in Latin America: An Emerging Tier-One National Security Priority." Carlisle Barracks, PA: Strategic Studies Institute, August 2012.

Hulse, Jane. "China's Expansion Into and U.S. Withdrawal from Argentina's Telecommunication and Space Industries and the Implications for U.S. National Security." Strategic Studies Institute, Carlisle Barracks, PA, 2007.

Pinheiro, Alvaro de Souza. "Narcoterrorism in Latin America: A Brazilian Perspective." Hurlburt Field, FL: JSOU, 2006.

Reaves, Jackie L. "The Emerging Threat of Illicit Drug Funding of Terrorist Organization." U.S. Army War College, Carlisle Barracks, PA, April 7, 2003.

Other Sources

Boote, John. "A Criminal Haven: The Tri-Border Area of South America." traccc.gmu.edu/pdfs/student_research/John%20Boote-%20A%20 Criminal%20Haven.pdf (accessed May 15, 2013).

Calderon, Horacio. "Organized Crime and Terrorism in the Triple Border Area." www.horaciocalderon.com (accessed May 27, 2013).

Castaneda, Sebastian. "South America Awake to the Risks of China Ties." *Asian Times*. http://www.atimes.com/atimes/China/MD21Ad01.htm (accessed April 8, 2013).

Central Intelligence Agency. "CIA and the War on Terrorism." http://www.cia.gov/news-information/cia-the-war-on-terrorism/terrorism-faqs.html (accessed May 15, 2013).

Ellis, Stephen. "West Africa's International Drug Trade." http://users.polisci.wisc.edu/schatzberg/ps362/Ellis2009.pdf (accessed May 15, 2013).

Forbes. "What Capitalists Should Know About State-Owned Enterprises." February 22, 2013. http://www.forbes.com/sites/hbsworkingknowledge/2013/02/22/what-capitalists-should-know-about-state-owned-enterprises (accessed May 15, 2013).

Gordon, Kate, Susan Lyon, Ed Paisley, and Sean Pool. "Rising to the Challenge: A Progressive U.S. Approach to China's Innovation and Competitiveness Policies." http://www.americanprogress.org/issues/2011/01/pdf/cjina_innovation.pdf (accessed May 15, 2013).

Hemmings, John. "Hedging: The Real U.S. Policy towards China." *The Diplomat*. May 13, 2013. http://thediplomat.com/the-editor/2013/05/13/hedging-the-real-u-s-policy-towards-china/ (accessed May 27, 2013).

Hoffman, Joshua T. "Tri-Border Area (TBA)." http://research.ridgway.pitt.edu/blog/2012/05/15/tri-border-area-tba/ (accessed May 10, 2013).

Jiang, Wenran. "The Danger for U.S.-China Ties." *The Diplomat*, October 1, 2011. http://thediplomat.com/2011/10/01/the-danger-for-us-china-ties/ (accessed May 27, 2013).

Mattlin, Mikael. "Chinese Strategic State-Owned Enterprises and Ownership Control." http://www.vub.ac.be/biccs/site/assets/files/apapers/Asia%20papers/Asia%20Paper%204(6).pdf (accessed May 15, 2013).

Swaine, Michael. "Avoiding U.S.-China Military Rivalry." *The Diplomat*. http://thediplomat.com/whats-next-china/avoiding-us-china-military-rivalry/ (accessed May 27, 2013).

Tiankai, Cui, and Pang Hanzhao. "China-U.S. Relations in China's Overall Diplomacy in the New Era," http://www.fmprc.gov.cn/eng/zxxx/t953682.htm (accessed May 27, 2013).

The White House. "Strategy to Combat Transnational Organized Crime: Definition." National Security Council. http://www.whitehouse.gov/administration/eop/nsc/transnational-crime/definition (accessed May 26, 2013).

Woetzel, Jonathan R. "Reassessing China's State-Owned Enterprises." http://www.mckinseyquarterly.com/Reassessing_Chinas_state_owned_enterprises_2149 (accessed May 15, 2013).